AN OUTDOORSMAN'S HEART

THE OUTDOORS THROUGH HIS EYES

BLAKE ALMA

© Copyright: An Outdoorsman's Heart
By Blake Alma, 2018
ISBN-13:
978-0692141274
ISBN-10:
0692141278
Library of Congress Control Number:
2018907116

The Outdoorsman's Art Media
Cincinnati, Ohio

All scripture from the King James Version

Cover graphics by
Steven Haught
Cover image by Steve Colyer
Edited by Noah Haught

TABLE OF CONTENTS

To my family, so that they may understand this child's broken heart.

AN OUTDOORSMAN'S DYNASTY

Like most people, when we were first approached by Blake Alma to appear on his radio and television show, his age is what caught our attention. We get asked to do a lot of media but cannot ever remember being asked by a 17-year-old who hosts his show and has written blogs and books for years. We said yes to the interviews and were even more impressed by Blake's knowledge of the outdoors and his grasp of important social issues and biblical knowledge.

Blake Alma is an impressive entrepreneur, an accomplished outdoorsman and a brother in Christ. He is everything that is right about America and everything we have tried to impress and encourage to full development. When we see the boldness and depth of this young man and others in our country like Kyle Kashuv, we are hopeful for the future of our republic.

Our family totally relates to the connection of the creation to one's spiritual and political beliefs. The revelation of what God has made speaks strongly to the people who are willing to notice and listen. This concept has driven the Robertson family, built our business, our platform through *Duck Dynasty*, and our current activism in our public debate for the future of our great country. We are Christians first and Americans second, for this country was founded for us to achieve in both of those realms. Blake Alma is the next generation to help guide Christians and Americans to what the founders had in mind when they sacrificed to build the United States of America.

In *An Outdoorsman's Heart*, Blake not only tells his story of how and why he fell in love with the outdoors, but lays out a logical and biblical approach to many of today's hot topic social issues. He is spot on in his approach and we couldn't agree more in his conclusions and assertions. There are not very many advanced and mature people who would tackle what Blake does in this book and he does it freshly, boldly, and biblically.

Like us, we hope you're impressed that such a young man so articulately describes the current state of affairs in America and in the outdoor industry. We encourage you to be more impressed that out future has some bright and biblically grounded people that will lead our nation once we are gone.

~ Phil & Alan Robertson,
Men of God, Outdoorsmen, and
Stars of *A&E's Duck Dynasty*

INTRODUCTION:

An Outdoorsman's Dream

There was once a boy with a dream, a dream that no other in the course of history has ever had. He would stop at nothing to accomplish that which he dreamed of. He began his pursuit and very slowly began to accomplish his goal, trying and trying and never giving up no matter what trials came his way. He learned throughout his journey that people were stubborn in their unrighteous ways. He found that people became vain in their imaginations and that their foolish hearts were darkened. People professed themselves to be wise, but they were fools. They changed the glory of his uncorruptible God into an image made like a corruptible man, to birds, four-footed beasts, and creeping things. They changed the truth of his God into a lie and worshipped and served the creature more than the Creator who is blessed forever.

And because of the boy's zeal and passion many thought to harm the boy and prevent him from pursuing that which was right. He kept immersing as many he could in an experience, an experience that would maybe cleanse the minds of millions. He wanted to show people the creation of the world so that they would be without an excuse to deny his God. The creation that the boy dreamed of sharing was given to bless mankind, to help them see that which was important in life. He wanted them to see the power, glory, love, mercy, and grace of his incorruptible God. When they heard of the boy's almighty God, they glorified him not as God, neither were they thankful for His creation. The boy's heart broke. His dream began to fade away for people butchered what he loved. He hoped that all would come to see and treasure all of God's creation so that they could see and come to Him. The boy's dream became lost. But then he learned not all of mankind was lost in their imaginations. A very select few loved his God's creation just as much as he did. The boy rejoiced. The boy took his knowledge of God's creation and attempted to share what His creation truly meant to this select people. Many already believed in God's existence, power, and glory, but there is so much more to the doctrines of creation.

He began to share the wonders and the grace of his God through all his platforms and his party accepted him while others hated him. The boy's generation came to despise him and his God. In fact, they proclaimed there was no God. But the boy remembered that he was not ashamed of the gospel of Christ. For the invisible things of God from the creation of the world are clearly seen, being understood by all things that are made so that they are without excuse to believe in Him!

This is how the boy saw God's creation.

THIS IS THE OUTDOORS THROUGH HIS EYES,

THE GATEWAY TO

HIS OUTDOORSMAN'S HEART!

CHAPTER 1:

AN OUTDOORSMAN'S STORY

It was September 24th of 2000 and it was a beautiful autumn day. The sun was shining and the birds were singing. My mother and father were outside hunting on that opening day of the deer season. My mother, over nine months pregnant, felt a kick within her womb. And then bam, her water broke. My parents were out in the heart of the woods with no cell phone signal and the car miles away from them. Henceforth, my dad used his wilderness survival skills and found a way to have his wife give birth right then and there, in the awe of creation. My dad used his survival knife to cut the umbilical cord. For all mothers give birth to a child, but not this mom, she gave birth to an outdoor legend. His name was BLAKE.

That entire story above is actually made up. What really happened is that my mom was in a hospital bed and out came Blake. The first thing he saw was his father with deer blood all over his camo outfit. Nope, that didn't happen either. I was born just like everyone else.

Well anyways, I was born at Bethesda North Hospital in Montgomery, Ohio on September 24, 2000 at 8:00 PM eastern, which was two days after deer opening season in Ohio. So yep, born to be an outdoorsman. Okay, I wasn't outdoorsy until I was twelve, but still, it's cool.

My dad was born and raised in Northern Michigan in the middle of nowhere. My father grew up in a house in the woods. The nearest Walmart was about twenty-five miles away. So, it sounds like he was a country boy raised to be an outdoorsman, right? Nope, even though he likes the outdoors, hunting and trapping isn't something he really ever pursued. My grandpa, liked to fish so my dad also liked to fish, but is it not his favorite thing to do. My dad actually was quite good with computers, so he pursued being an IT professional.

My mom was born in Alabama and raised in both Florida and Illinois. My mom really never told me about what she did as a child, but I do know what she ended up pursuing: teaching Elementary kids. Both my parents attended Pensacola Christian College, but they did not meet there. They met after being offered teaching jobs in Cincinnati, Ohio at Central Baptist Schools. My mom taught Elementary kids and my dad taught computer stuff. My mom and dad met when they both became volleyball coaches at the school. In February of 2000, my parents got married and later had me.

Once my "marvelous" birth occurred, they moved out of the city and into the suburbs of Sharonville, Ohio, my beloved hometown. We moved to a calm and quiet neighborhood. We had about a half-acre of land with a house that had three bedrooms. Our backyard was amazing! It was surrounded by woods and covered by a huge 80-foot red oak tree. It was a wonderful backyard. The wildlife in the yard was abundant. There were squirrels, chipmunks, rabbits, birds, raccoons, opossums, foxes, and deer. It was just plain wonderful. I grew up in that home and my outdoor origins began in that backyard.

Being an only child was wonderful, for a whole whopping year that is. My oldest brother was born just about three weeks after my first birthday. My brother entered the world of Blake. Blake's world was so perfect, like a beautiful stack of building blocks, until my little brother would knock it over. But that's what little brothers do. Well, he wasn't necessarily my little brother; he came out over ten pounds! He has always been taller than me. I am currently 5'10 and he is about 6' 4. It is funny, we go out in public and everyone thinks he is older than me. Not cool y'all, not cool! My face is obviously more mature and not to mention better looking.

Anyway, just he and I in the Alma family

forever. Nope, out came another dude in 2003. Then another guy in 2004. My mom was just popping them out! My dad, my mom, and four little dudes by the time I was four years old.

So when 2005 rolled around, I determined that I would be a he-man woman-hater, like some little kid who thought that girls were yuck and had cooties. That wasn't a good thing when you are just going to new church, trying to make new friends. Church was my only social time because I was homeschooled, which turned out to be a huge blessing in my life.

At our church, I ended up making a "club" called Captains versus Robots. Captain represented the dudes and Robots represented the girls. It was like a "who is cooler competition," boys or girls. Boys are way cooler, but the girls didn't think that. Therefore, it just ended up being a long competition between girls and boys.

During this time, I didn't have a lot of hobbies. The iPod didn't exist, thankfully, so I just played with action figures. I was also into spies and secret agents.

I took that a little too far. Way too far. I spied on random people. It is kind of weird when I look back and think about it, I even started recruiting people to "spy" for me it. I was already little businessman, but a weird one. I even made up fake identities and stuff. I seriously invaded people's business. It was just weird. I am glad those days are over.

Let's not forget the infamous Xbox 360. When the gaming console came out, my dad and his generation loved it. He played this darn game called Halo like all the time. He even got me and my brothers playing it with him at a freakishly young age.

I mean sure, I don't mind video games, but I am not going to play more than an hour straight. Just a big old waste of time. I'd now rather be out pursuing the art of game hunting or practicing survival skills. It is so much more fun. However, at that time I didn't know anything about the outdoor world. I just did whatever my family did. I think I played it 15 hours a week. Just wasted time. I only wish I knew about the outdoors then.

Oh wait! My very first fishing trip. Our church had a father-son camping trip. Me, my dad, and my "little" brother went. I believe I was five or six years old at the time. The camping site was about 100 miles north of where we lived and there was a lake at the site. Of course, we went fishing. I only caught one lousy bluegill, while my brother caught a huge catfish that we ended up eating. My dad caught absolutely nothing. It was rather humorous. I don't remember much about the trip but for the most part it was enjoyable.

As time flew by, my life just became more interesting. In late 2006, my mom was again pregnant with the fifth child. It was a girl! When my mom and dad told me it was a girl, I actually cried because I wanted another baby brother. It changed our lives when she was born in June of 2007. We now had a little girl in the family.

Around my oldest sister's birth, we were renovating the house by adding a new bedroom! We had a porch on the side of the house where me and my siblings would play with a sandbox and stuff. I loved that porch. Oddly enough, that porch ended up becoming my mom and dad's bedroom. It took a few months for it to be built and it is one of those things I distinctly remember about my childhood. I even made a hundred bucks for helping around for a few minutes. It was great. As far as I can remember, my dad has always had a passion for fireworks. He decided to take his passion and turn it into a successful business. He made the mortar tubes that firework shells go into. He didn't start doing it full time until 2015.

In 2009 my mother popped out another girl. Shocker, right? Two more followed that one… so I was the oldest of 8 and we were all homeschooled.

MY TEEN LIFE

I have had one weird teen life. At eleven I entered the 7th grade, which is cool and all, but being the youngest you do get picked on. I was already going through a rough time leaving my childhood church and going to a new one. Literally a new church, as we are some of the founding members of that church. We still go there today. I am the first teen to go through the teen group from start to graduation.

Anyway, it was bit rough going to teen Sunday school and to youth activities. Just getting picked on about weird stuff bro. Weird stuff... stuff that I was very oblivious to back then. Yeah, exactly...

I dreamed about being the oldest kid in the group, so that one day I could be the "dope" kid. Well, I was the oldest in that group and it wasn't all that great. I like to say that during my time in teen group I went through these five stages:

- My first year or two was awkward but with no doubt the best year and I will tell you why in a moment.

- Our awesome teen leader then left the group and it just fell apart. Many teens left.

- Our pastor tried to take over but it just wasn't his passion.

- We got a new youth leader who was only like twenty-two and was only the youth leader to get the pastor's daughter. This was the majority of my teen years and it just sucked! He didn't care about the group and only wanted the pastor's daughter. He got her, and they left almost immediately after marriage! I was in 11th grade by then.

- And currently, we have a new leader who is great! The teen group has been forged to what it once was, and I was the oldest of the bunch.

So, the church teen group wasn't all that great, but I didn't tell you all of this to pity me. Because of this not-so-great teen group, it gave me the time and passion to pursue the outdoors and not focus on what my fellow teens thought about me. If it was an amazing teen group and I was best friends with everyone in the group, I would never have been who I am today! I am incredibly grateful to that teen group and my church for that.

Now, you may be thinking "Why was my first year the best year if everyone pestered you?" I went to a couple of teen camps that year and one of them changed my life.

THE FISHING EXPERIENCE THAT CHANGED IT ALL!

As I write this, I shed great tears of joyful memories. Writing about this moment is just wonderful. It was summer of 2013 and I went to a Christian teen camp in Indiana just right on the border of Ohio. As I have already mentioned, I was picked on, and even more so during boy's swim time. I got dunked and tossed. It wasn't fun and I have not gone swimming in a pool since.

Well, one man, one camp counselor had such zeal to reintroduce kids back into the outdoors that he asked scrawny little me if I wanted to go fishing, noticing that I was bullied. Little did he know that that one question would change my life. I said yes and we went fishing at a little creek. We caught a lot of small fish, like bluegill and bass. I had an awesome time fishing with him all week.

Camp came to an end and I said goodbye to him and never saw him again. (Just kidding, saw him again but it wasn't till a few years later.) But at that camp I found a great pleasure in God's creation when

Bryan May introduced me to the sport of fishing. Because one man I didn't really know took me fishing, my life was revolutionized!

When I saw him again I had already became a radio host and author (I hadn't become a TV host yet). When I saw him I ran up to him and said, "I got some stories to tell you!" I probably cried too. Man, that was an awesome moment in my life.

I like to sit down and think about this moment often. If Bryan had never taken me fishing, where would I be at today? I highly doubt that I would be an outdoorsman, and I can never express the amount of gratitude I have for Bryan for taking me on the quick fishing trip that revolutionized my life.

THE NEXT STEP

I could write another book about my life experiences and what has happened since that moment. But for the sake of getting straight to this book's point, I will attempt (and probably fail) to quickly tell you the events after my life-changing fishing experience.

An Outdoorsman's Story

After falling in deep love with fishing, I ventured into other outdoor activities. Since I lived in a small house with ten people and I lived in a neighborhood, I was pretty limited to the outdoor things I could do on our property. I most certainly couldn't deer hunt but what I could do was start fires, make primitive traps, and practice bushcraft/wilderness skills. Hence, I did just that. While pursing backyard outdoor activities, I decided to write a short, kind of goofy book about the skills I had learned. I named this book *The Outdoorsmen's Bible*.

Of course, I was thirteen, maybe even twelve years old when I started work on this project and I was no wordsmith. I did give it my best shot. I ran into so many hiccups that I almost trashed the book, but I am so happy I didn't. I finished the book and it was a thirteen-year-old masterpiece. Just kidding, it is actually quite horrible as I look back on it now. I then tried to find a way to publish the book, but I didn't have any knowledge or money to know how to publish anything. To add to that, it was hand written and it needed to be typed up. I gave up trying to get it published for quite some time.

Time flew by again, and I ran into someone that knew how to get a book published. Because of that, I got it published in December of 2014. When it ran for sale, I thought I would sell tons of copies. Well, I didn't. Turns out, I was a horrible writer back then and nobody really cared for a young teen's advice on what little outdoor experiences he had. But that book lead to me writing several more books and encouraged me to start a blog. *The Outdoorsmen's Bible* is discontinued because I am so ashamed of my former writing. The only way to get your hands on that book is to listen to it on audio, which isn't as bad to me.

On May 27, 2015, I started a blog called "The Art of an Outdoorsman," (which is "The Conservative Sportsman" today.) It was a simple blogger page with some of the outdoorsy things I was up too. Writing my blog gave me better writing skills and enabled me to write freelance for various online outdoor sites and even magazines. The first online site I began writing for was "Survival Life." I got paid to write for them too, and for a teenager, I was making quite a pretty penny. It was a very enjoyable experience that lead me to becoming an outdoor radio host.

April of 2016 rolls around and WRVO Radio Network 1 reached out to me and asked me if I wanted my own outdoor radio show!!! I thought it was a scam or something of that matter at first. But it was legit! Tuesday, May 31st, 2016 was my premiere date for my first show. Oh man, did that turn my career around. Let's talk about that quickly.

After my failed experience of my first book, I kept my young age a secret. I didn't tell anyone on my blog or articles about my age in fear that no one would listen to me. My first co-host on my radio show convinced me that it would be good to mention that I was a 15-year-old hosting a radio show. Apparently, people found that impressive. I was very humble then, but not so much now unfortunately. I didn't necessarily think my age was that impressive as I enjoyed my job. I tried to never let it get to my head, but I heard that I was the only teenager ever to host an outdoor radio show. And my very humble self thought that was pretty dope.

The show kicked off not because I was good at it, (because I wasn't,) but because of my age. I began receiving so much vocal support it just took off. I started getting friend requests on Facebook from people that I did not know at all, made some amazing connections, and new outdoor friends. It was awesome. On the show, we interviewed all types of guests, from the average hunter to celebrity outdoor icons. It was, and still is, an amazing adventure.

I've got to admit, when an adult or someone asks me if I have a job, it is a pretty awesome feeling to answer that question and tell them what it is. But then it turns them off when they hear it is about shooting animals in the face and drowning worms. But still… Nowadays, I just tell random people when they ask about my job that I work in media to avoid being too cocky and telling them my life story which gets kind of tiring after telling it all the time. And now, I am writing about it! Erg…

After a year of hosting the radio show, I wanted

to venture into other outdoor media outlets and one of those outlets was outdoor television. Now, I know what you're thinking, "Everyone these days has an outdoor show," which is absolutely correct. So, I decided to take on the outdoor TV industry from another angle. Since I already had a background with hosting an outdoor talk show, I asked myself, "What if I started an outdoor talk show?!?! Like 'The Tonight Show,' but outdoorsy!" But since my teenage budget wouldn't allow me to have celebrities fly into my great outdoors studio, I thought I would just do an outdoor talk show with guests on the phone. I then ran my idea by the Hunt Channel and they loved it.

Then my precious outdoor experience was born. "The Outdoor Experience with Blake Alma" premiered on the Hunt Channel Monday, May 22nd at 10 PM eastern. Can't even begin to articulate what that has done for me. It is pretty amazing and fun stuff. Through the show, I have been able to interview so many amazing people. Phil Robertson, Michael Waddell, Jim & Eva Shockey, Ted Nugent, Jase Robertson, Nick Mundt, and Chad Mendes are just to name a few. What an awesome experience! (No pun intended!)

That is pretty much my story. I am here now writing this book and readers might wonder, "Why is Blake writing this book? Is it to praise himself for his accomplishments?" That is hardly the case. It was not because of my own merit that I am here today but because of my gracious Creator. It is simply my faith that has driven this journey. The outdoors is so much more than a hobby or an experience. I said the following in an interview on a local TV network:

"Even though the outdoors is a place of enjoyment and pleasure, it is also a place that shows the glory and wonder of a Creator. There is no place I'd rather be than in a place that shows me the attributes of my Creator."

O how I believe that today more than ever. The old hymn, "This is my Father's World," my favorite hymn, says it best. Read these words:

An Outdoorsman's Story

"This is my Father's world

And to my listening ears

All nature sings, and round me rings

The music of the spheres

This is my Father's world

The birds their carols raise

The morning light, the lily white

Declare their Maker's praise

This is my Father's world

I rest me in the thought

Of rocks and trees, of skies and seas

His hand the wonders wrought

This is my Father's world

Oh, let me never forget

That though the wrong seems oft so strong

God is the ruler yet

This is my Father's world

Why should my heart be sad?

The Lord is king, let the heavens ring

AN OUTDOORSMAN'S HEART

God reigns, let the earth be glad

This is my Father's world
He shines in all that's fair
In the rustling grass, I hear him pass
He speaks to me everywhere

In the rustling grass, I hear him pass
He speaks to me everywhere"

What a powerful song. It gives me goose bumps! In the rustling grass, I too, hear Him pass. My outdoorsman's heart will not be sad when I walk in the midst of creation to remember that God is indeed the ruler yet. I am a kid that receives so much backlash and hate for this faith and my love for hunting. All that seems lost fades away when I am lost in Him and His creation.

But when I step out of His church and His creation and back into the world; my heart does become sad. When I turn on the TV or scroll through Facebook, all does seem lost. I have cried and mourned for all that is occurring in this once great nation. I said at my high school graduation, "Oh America, your vain and foolish follies are more than I can bear." And it truly is.

However, all hope is not lost. The outdoor industry is, in fact, the most conservative industry out there which brings a big grin to my face. However, our conservativism is not getting us to heaven. It is my faith in God that he sent His only Son to die on that rugged cross for my own sins and that he rose again three days later. It is not my own conservative moral merit that will enter me into the kingdom of God. I encourage you, my fellow outdoorsman, to consider all the works my God has made, the creation He has made for you, and how it proves His existence and His word. Accept Him into your outdoorsman's heart so that you can live for Him and go to His kingdom. I beg of you. We conservative outdoorsmen are the last of a dying breed and we cannot change the world on our own but through Christ. There is simply nothing better than a Christian outdoorsman!

Let my faith never go out void, O God!

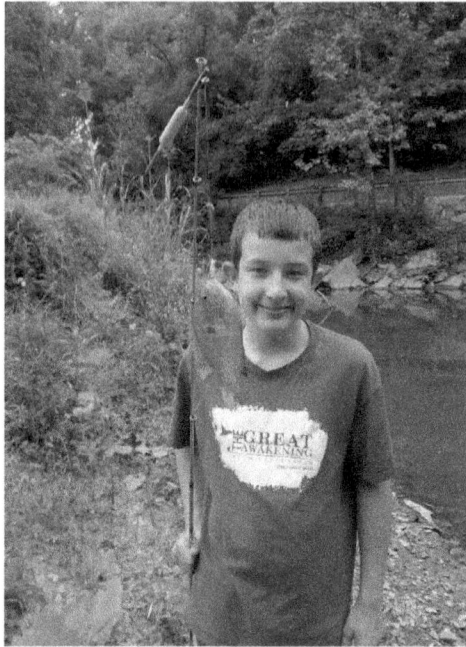

Blake's fishing trip that changed his life (2013)

TV show's logo

The
Outdoorsman's
Art
Radio Show
with Blake Alma
and
Jackson Hartley

Radio show's logo

Blake interviewing Ted Nugent

Blake interviewing Jim Shockey

Blake interviewing Chad Mendes

Blake hosting his TV Show

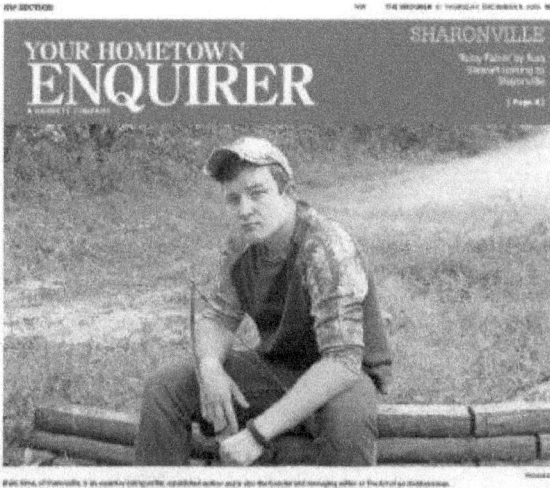

Blake's first time in the papers (2016)

BLAKE ALMA
17-YEAR-OLD RADIO AND TV HOST
LOCAL 12

Blake on local news network talking about his love for outdoors (2017)

MAKING HIS OWN WAY

NEW THIS MORNING
SHARONVILLE TEEN WRITES BOOK, HOSTS TV SHOW
FORECASTS DISCLAIMER IN YOUR SIDE NEWS TICKER IS SPONSORED BY LAROSAS, JEEP, 6:10 60°

Blake's passion being discussed on local media (2017)

Blake graduating high school (2018)

Outline artwork of the book's cover (by Steve Coyler)

NEWS   VIDEO   SHOT SHOW 2018   REVIEWS   MORE ▾

Meet a 16-Year-Old Survival Expert

Tim MacWelch

Blake featured on *OutdoorHub* written by *New York Times* Best-selling author, Tim MacWelch.

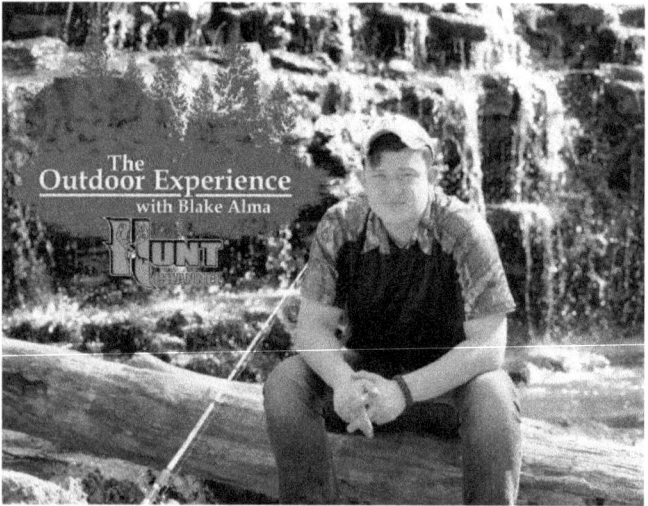

The
Outdoor Experience
with Blake Alma

Blake chatting about his book on *Cincy Lifestyle*.

CHAPTER 2:

AN OUTDOORSMAN'S DOCTRINE

THE DOCTRINE OF CREATION

Although one may find it weird that a teenager would come up with his own name of a hidden doctrine in the Bible and in creation, this is still truthful and helpful to the outdoorsman.

The fool has said in his heart there is no God. One is simply a fool when they deny the existence of God. All of creation proves His existence. Let me put this into very simple terms in the very likely event you run into an atheist vegan or even an outdoorsman.

Atheism is the belief of no God. Bawaaaa…

funny. Then explain how the earth was made?

"Well by evolution of course," the atheist scoffs.

What is Evolution? Let me tell you… Evolution is the belief that there was nothing, and nothing happened to nothing and then nothing magically exploded for no reason. This creating everything, and then a bunch of everything magically rearranged itself for no reason, whatsoever, into self-replicating bits which then turned into plants, then animals, and then later humans. Right… that makes perfect sense!

Another fact is that we do not just see things poof out of nowhere by accident. Let's say I invited you into my home. You walk into my home and tell me my house is super nice. I then reply, "Yeah man, it's crazy bro. It just poofed here by chance one day. Came out of nowhere. It is pretty epic!" You'd think I were a nutjob. That is precisely how atheists think the outdoors is made. It just poofed. Everything about atheism is not at all logical.

However, God's existence and a six/24-hour day creation isn't all that logical either. And that is why it is called faith. I want you to sit down and really think about the Bible and it's contents then think about evolution and it's rubbish. After you do that, tell me which one is more requires more faith. Think about how the Bible proves itself through not only the outdoors, but through science and even how the human body functions so impressively. Tell me then how that happened by mere chance of two atoms making a big bang.

When someone is born, they are not born an atheist. One determines this sometime later in their life because this or that negative thing happened. Most atheists conclude there is no God because something bad happened in their life or in general. You don't wake up one day and say there is no God. They think that since God is a God of love and this bad thing happened, then God must not be real. May I remind you, that God is indeed a God of love. However, we fall so very short of His standards that we sin on an hourly basis. So, He has every right to punish you... and the fact that you and I are still breathing shows His love and mercy. I mean, if you treated me horribly, defied me every minute, and I have absolute dominion over you, you would not be here. It is absolutely foolish to deny His existence, as your opinion does not change fact.

Now, I say all this with a zealous love. I am passionate for my God and His creation that he made to prove His existence. Oh, you don't believe me that the outdoors was created to show God's reality. Let me show you what the Bible says.

My favorite Bible verse states, *"For the invisible things of him from the creation of the world are clearly seen, being understood by the things that are made, even his eternal power and Godhead; so that they are without excuse..."* Romans 1:20

Let's break this down. What are *"the invisible things of Him"*? They are simply the air, atoms, and microorganisms that we cannot see but know exist. *"The creation of the world"* is a really easy one. What is the creation in this world? The outdoors is! This little part of the verse is saying that the air, atoms, microorganisms, and the outdoors is easy to see and to acknowledge as real.

"Being understood by the things that are made"

means that you understand that a house, building, machine, and everything has to be made/built or else it cannot exist. So far, it is very simple.

"Even his eternal power and Godhead" is just a bit harder to understand but it means that you know everything is made and cannot just be made by accident. Then that means the air, atoms, outdoors, etc., must be made by God, or else it wouldn't exist. Since everything else has to be constructed and can't simply make itself, then God had to make all those things too. Henceforth, you know that you *"are without excuse"* to deny God's existence and power. It is pretty straightforward doctrine.

I hope you understand that one of the main purposes of the outdoors is to prove God's existence. I can't talk about that enough here, or on my shows.

Another attribute the outdoors provides is showing God's glory and power. The outdoors praises the qualities of God. Let's quickly see what the Bible says on this.

Psalms 19:1 ~ *The heavens declare the glory of God;*

and the firmament sheweth his handywork.

This is perhaps one of the most famous verses that states how His creation shows God's glory.

Job 37:14 ~ *Hearken unto this, O Job: stand still, and consider the wondrous works of God.*

This is one of my favorite verses in the Old Testament. If you read the book of Job, you will learn that Job was a very rich man that ended up losing everything he ever had so that God could once more prove the devil wrong. God tested Job's response and he did that which was right. Elihu, a dear friend of Job, was telling him this verse. He told Job to stop what he was doing (he was mourning his loses), take a second, and think of all the wonderous works of God. When you are in a time of struggle, stop thinking of the negative and think about God's wonderful creation. Fred Bear once said, *"Immerse yourself in the outdoor experience, it will cleanse your soul and make you a better person."* I base my life upon this experience and I assure you this is true.

Psalms 8:3-4a ~ *When I consider thy heavens, the work of thy fingers, the moon and the stars, which thou hast ordained; What is man, that thou art mindful of him?*

When you think of all of God's wonders, it sets your mind on the power of God. It shows you we are nothing and He is everything.

Psalms 148:7-13 ~ *Praise the LORD from the earth, ye dragons, and all deeps: Fire, and hail; snow, and vapours; stormy wind fulfilling his word: Mountains, and all hills; fruitful trees, and all cedars: Beasts, and all cattle; creeping things, and flying fowl: Kings of the earth, and all people; princes, and all judges of the earth: Both young men, and maidens; old men, and children: Let them praise the name of the LORD: for his name alone is excellent; his glory is above the earth and heaven.*

Every single piece of creation shows that God's glory is above all things!

Job 12:7-10 ~ *But ask now the beasts, and they shall teach thee; and the fowls of the air, and they shall tell thee: Or speak to the earth, and it shall teach thee: and the fishes of the sea shall declare unto thee. Who knoweth not in all these that the hand of the LORD hath wrought this? In whose hand is the soul of every living thing, and the breath of all mankind.*

From the fish of the sea to the beasts of the earth, it all shows His infinite power.

Isaiah 43:20a ~ *The beast of the field shall honour me, the dragons and the owls: because I give waters in the wilderness, and rivers in the desert...*

The cattle, owls, the vast wilderness, and even dinosaurs honor God's glory.

Those are just a few verses that touch on God's glory and power. The outdoors was given to rest your mind in God's glory and fix your mind on godly desires. But that's not all; the outdoors also shows God's love and mercy.

You know, God could have stripped us from all the glorious scenery and pursuits of the outdoors. He could have done so. We have fallen short to the glory of God and disobeyed every single one of His commandments. But meanwhile, God showed his love toward us to allow us to enjoy all the benefits of His creation and that I'll never forget.

His mercy is beyond comprehension. He has the very right to strike us dead for He created us and then we fell to our own greed. But yet God gives His love toward us, and while we were yet sinners, Christ died for us as it says in Romans. It is unbelievably mind boggling that God would send His only Son to die for this selfish, worthless, outdoorsman's heart.

CHAPTER 3:

AN OUTDOORSMAN'S SIN

I firmly believe that outdoorsmen have more morals than any other party. That is absolutely wonderful. I have found that 98% of outdoorsmen and women are, in fact, conservative and hold to traditional values. The majority of the outdoor industry would come to agree that there is a God, that abortion is murder, that homosexuality is sin, that liberalism is a disorder, and that Trump is a great president! As I have stated before, none of those things will get us to heaven, only our trust and faith in God will. However, that is a great place to begin.

This industry is far from perfect, unfortunately.

AN OUTDOORSMAN'S HEART

There are so many issues among us that bring me to my knees, and since we're abnormally conservative we should know better. I always like to start off with a positive fact and then go into negative because the Bible works that way too. The outdoors is like a brotherhood. We are all in this awesome race to get as many kids and people outdoors to enjoy it and cherish it. We all have that same great bond running through our veins. Most of us get along with one another because we see the purpose of the outdoors. However, there have been times where we get caught up in our pride and claim that we are a better hunter or fisherman than someone else. I hate it more when hunters fight against hunters than when a vegan harasses a hunter for their right to hunt. We should act better than the opposing party. Let me take on this topic as I step on some shoes and chew on my own shoe leather.

Hunters argue about entirely unnecessary things. One of them being that we think we are a better hunter than another fellow hunter. First off, there is no real way to measure that. Some may say that Jim

An Outdoorsman's Sin

Shockey is the greatest hunter alive while others may argue that Donald Trump Jr. is. I assure you that there are better hunters than both Jim and Donald Trump Jr. that are just keeping a low profile. I have found that we hunters have measured that one is a better hunter by fame. Fame is just people knowing of your name, it is not that fact that they are better than you at a certain activity. I kid you not; I have seen people argue that they are a better hunter because they are a pro-staff member for so and so. I hate to break it to you buddy, but your 20% discount doesn't make you better hunter. It may give you more credentials than the other hunter, but it doesn't mean you are better. It is absolutely comical to think so. We need to humble ourselves for the sake of Christ and passing the outdoors onto others. What city slicker would want to be an outdoorsman if the only thing he/she sees us do is argue about who is better? This pointless argument will destroy this industry if we don't stop it now!

More nonsense is when hunters get all worked up about using a crossbow. Who cares guys? Why does it hurt you that someone else uses a crossbow while you use a compound? Both a compound bow and crossbow are modern weapons and are much easier to use than a traditional bow. So, you insulting someone for using a crossbow while you use a compound bow is quite hypocritical, as you are also using a technologically advanced weapon. Now if you use a traditional bow, more power to you, but it is not your right or concern to harp another hunter for the weapon they choose. So, I hope you understand this point I am making.

Hunters who use crossbows are generally people who can't draw a compound because of health or age. Most crossbow users are underaged and cannot pull back a compound. They could also be older in age and lack the strength of their youth. Another reason could be that they are disabled and lack the capability to draw a compound. Another probable reason, and it is a little awkward to say, is one may be out of shape, which I think is the most common reason. What is great about the outdoors though is that any size, height, weight, race, or color can enjoy the great outdoor experience. If you need to use a crossbow to enjoy the outdoors, I fully endorse that, and I applaud you for going outdoors despite your conditions. So, when one harasses another hunter for using a different weapon, it is ridiculous and unnecessary. When a hunter and another hunter argues, it hurts our party and enables the left to infiltrate us more easily. You are helping the vegans and antihunters when you harass a fellow brother in the outdoors. I advise you to knock it off as it is entirely uncool, and no outdoorsman needs more negative in his life, especially from the same outdoor party.

Another scenario is when hunters get aggressive with other hunters for baiting deer. Now, if it is illegal in your state, don't bait deer. Duh! But if your state allows it and you are comfortable with taking advantage of it, go for it. I have no issues with baiting deer. Just like the crossbow issue, it is a pride thing. It is a hunter thinking that they are a better hunter than another because they don't bait deer and the other does. Again, it is a none of your business ordeal. It doesn't matter at all if you want to bait deer and it's legal. Please do! Enjoy that great outdoor experience and don't let someone take you away from doing so by saying baiting deer is for losers. It isn't. If you use deer scents/lures, you are baiting deer. If you are using a food plot, you are baiting deer. If you are using anything that lures in deer, you are baiting.

I understand that you may think that baiting deer spreads more disease to deer. If there is a disease among deer, it will spread with or without deer baiting. Deer eat from the same food source. So, a natural food source will also hold the previous feeding deer's bacteria and pass it on to the next muncher. This is an invalid argument then. Also, baiting deer with corn piles and a food plot are the same thing. Sure, one may grow out of the earth while the other is poured onto the earth, but they are both food and deer will continue returning to either baiting source. Next time you encounter a deer corn baiter, just smile and admire the fact that they love the same sport that you do.

Of course, people sometimes argue about the

better brand. Most hunting harassment happens on social media. I think social media is better for the outdoors than bad as it brings people together to share the same passion. But when there is good, there is also bad. Let's just use the camo industry as an example. There are tons of different camo brands out there and the two biggest are Realtree and Mossy Oak. At this moment, Realtree is my favorite, as I like the patterns better than other brands. But that is just me and my preference. If you like Mossy Oak or some other brand, sweet bro! I don't care. I am not going to debate you or get in a heated argument as to why I think Realtree is better. It is just my preference. Every hunter is different and we all like different things. This also applies to all sorts of outdoor related product not just camo. Everyone is trying to make money off of this industry, but we must simply remember that the outdoors isn't about money. It is about God's glory and passing it on to the next generation to enjoy. I don't care what product you use as long it isn't sinful or representing something that is against the Bible. I am just simply happy that you enjoy the outdoors just like me. I cannot repeat that enough. We are the last of a dying breed and we must do everything we can to keep the heritage alive for generations to come.

Alright, so let's jump off the harassment band wagon as I think you understand the point. Now, this next issue is an issue across all industries, not just ours. It is the fact that sex sells. I hate even bringing this issue up as I really don't even know how to tackle it. Yes, normal guys are turned on by a girl in camo. There is nothing wrong at all when a girl wears camo and wants to get outdoors. I love that. I think the big issue here is us guys. Have we become that idiotic that we make even the outdoors perverted? We have butchered the outdoors, one of God's finest creations, to fit our own perverted imaginations! How awful of us. We, the outdoorsmen, are better than this. PETA uses sex all the time for their nasty cause. But how are we any better than them if we do the same thing? There is no denying that lust is one of man's greatest issues. Why can't we just get over this so that our kids have the common decency to respect

God's creation. Both the outdoors and women. I could belabor this topic for an entire chapter, but I won't. I know that you know that lust is wrong and that we have corrupted the wonderful creation God because of our perverted thoughts and actions. We must focus on that which is right, or else our opposing party will win our children and outdoor heritage.

CHAPTER 4:

AN OUTDOORSMAN'S HERITAGE

My fellow teens have fallen into a misconception.

The sadness it brings my heart that my generation has little to no morals is unbearable. While eating Tide Pods and snorting condoms, they proclaim the answer to violence is banning the one item that prevents violence. They want to bring a liberal revolution to this great nation as they try to figure out what bathroom to use. They shout from the mountains that there is no God and that it is cool to kill an unborn child. They wave their rainbow flags down the streets, taking pride in their abominations. They hold signs that state "*Screw* Trump" and that white people have nothing to be proud of. I have had the great pleasure of never meeting the infamous David Hogg, a fellow seventeen-year-old who does not speak for me. Oh, my fellow peers, who taught you these vain and untruthful follies? I first scoff, and then mourn for your perverted agendas. But then a beam of light shines through the clouds as I remember my fellow outdoorsmen and their children, and that they raised them in traditional godly ways.

There is no greater joy than when I see a young child with his dad at a hunting expo. The smile it brings to me is like nothing else. Knowing that he will know the difference between right and wrong is comforting. It is your child, outdoorsman, that will be last to fight for the good in this great nation. Remember that!

If you are an outdoorsman, you need to get your kid outdoors as early as you are comfortable with. I am not going to tell you how to raise your own kid besides the fact that you need to teach them about God, America, Family and the outdoors! Simple enough if you start them young. If you don't teach them young, but you wait until they are older, they will likely already be sucked into the mainstream world of tech and foolishness. Of course, better late then never though.

Again, you raising your own kid is your business. I am seventeen at the time of this book's publishing and I obviously don't have any kids. However, I am the oldest of eight kids and do have a lot of experience with handling kids. I also have a lot of outdoor experiences for seventeen-year-old. So, let me combine what little knowledge I have of the two and see how you can get a kid back outdoors.

As we all know, times are changing, and the use of technology – especially by youth – is increasing at an unprecedented rate.

That said, I believe the outdoors is greater than anything ever invented by man – yes, even smartphones. The Creator gave us the outdoors to keep, treasure, and enjoy. Decades ago, nearly every child loved playing outside and lifting rocks to find worms. Now, technology and devices have largely taken the place of spending time outdoors for our youth, and for that reason, I think the outdoors is needed in a child's life now more than ever.

Is it not an outdoorsman's duty to pass their skill down to the next generation? Today, the great art of an outdoorsman is dying, and it is up to us to revive it. Thankfully, the outdoors can be taught in so many different ways – including with the help of technology and smartphones.

I am truly convinced that the most effective way today to revive the dying art of an outdoorsman is to use what youth love most – technology. In fact, today the outdoors should be easier to teach than it was a 100 years ago. We have so many tools that we can use to teach others.

YouTube is a great teaching tool. Videos can easily be made and uploaded to YouTube using a simple smartphone. You don't need all the fancy editing equipment to do videos, either. Use what you have to make them, upload to YouTube, and then share on social media. Teens love watching videos, so use that platform. Try to be funny too.

Social media is also a fantastic way to reach others. My generation loves social media, like Instagram, Facebook and Snapchat. Make posts sharing your love for the outdoors and sharing the wonders therein. Before I had ever gone hunting, I would see my friends post their kills on Facebook. Boy, did it make me want to go hunting more. Social media can encourage outdoorsmen to teach one another and teach those who know little.

Blogging is another way to reach people. Not only can you educate people, but you could also turn it into a profit by selling ad space. Blogging is easy, it just takes time to build your site and audience. I have two blogs myself, one with more than 160k Facebook likes. You can use Facebook as a tool to build an audience. Making a Facebook page and group is a great way to get started with building your audience. You can then go to blogger.com to make a free blog.

Of course, taking a kid hiking, camping, fishing,

hunting, shooting or even trapping, especially one who doesn't have parents who are "outdoorsy," is perhaps the most meaningful way to share your love for the outdoors. It will change that kid's life, as it changed mine!

Let me run by some ideas I have to take kids outdoors. If you have your own kids, maybe schedule a "playdate" with your kid's friend and do it outdoors. Like going fishing, camping, boating, or even visiting a park. Another idea is for you to get a hold of another buddy of yours that does outdoor activities. You can plan with them an outdoor activity with your whole family and kids. If you go to a church, you can plan a church kid's activity that is outdoors. I think a fishing trip or campout activity would be ideal for this. I was going to mention that you could be an outdoor teacher to kids by being a Boy Scout troop leader. But now, I really don't think that is a good idea. We will talk about that later. Anyway, there is a bucket load of things you can do to get kids outdoors and get them to want to go outside.

Because of that time so long ago, when Bryan May took me fishing, I am here writing you this book. If that wouldn't have happened, my life would be dramatically different. However, because it did occur, I too get to teach what Bryan taught me. So, I encourage you to take as many kids outside as possible.

If we all work together and teach this next generation the wonders of the outdoors, it will change this nation and make it stronger than ever before.

CHAPTER 5:

AN OUTDOORSMAN'S CONSERVATIVISM

If you know anything about me, it is the fact that I really like to talk about my political views. It does seem to me that 98% of outdoorsmen agree with what I say. The whole 2% of outdoorsmen who are liberal are the oddballs of our party. Don't get me wrong, I love the fact that they get outdoors, but they don't hold the same moral values and that means being an outdoorsman then has no greater value than being a hobby. Yes, I am about to get politically incorrect and I am going to spend quite a bit of time here. I am going to start with issue number one. Here we go!

<u>ABORTION</u>

Oh, how I hate abortion more than anything else on this earth. Yes, anything! Why is that? It is the murder of an innocent child in the womb because the majority of the time the parent is too lazy to take care of him or her. Liberals deny that an unborn baby is living. But let me ask you, what disqualifies an unborn human as a living human being? Here are some liberal responses:

Liberal: Because it doesn't know it is alive…
Me: So, that means a special needs child, someone with dementia, someone in a coma, or heck, even someone who is just sleeping isn't alive? Good logic…

Liberal: Because it can't live on its own…
Me: So then it is okay to kill a *born* child? They can't survive without their parent or guardian. Umm, with that logic you should go to prison.

Liberal: Because I didn't give him/her permission to be in my body...

Me: The second you decided to have sex is the second you gave permission for the child to enter your body. I hate to break it to you, because maybe your dad didn't teach you, but sex isn't for pleasure. It is to reproduce and have children. Maybe you shouldn't have sex outside of marriage like the Bible says... there's an idea. Is it worth killing a human being for few minutes of sinful pleasure?

Liberal: Well, the Bible doesn't say abortion is murder...

Me: *"Lo, children are an heritage of the Lord: and the fruit of the womb is his reward."* - Psalm 127:3

"For thou hast possessed my reins: thou hast covered me in my mother's womb. I will praise thee; for I am fearfully and wonderfully made: marvellous are thy works; and that my soul knoweth right well." - Psalm 139:13-14

"Before I formed thee in the belly I knew thee; and before thou camest forth out of the womb I sanctified thee, and I ordained thee a prophet unto the nations."
- Jeremiah 1:5

Those are just a few verses that talk about the human being God formed in the womb. The verse above clarifies that an unborn child is, in fact, a human being. Don't believe me? Research some verses on your own that talk about life in the womb.

"Thou shall not kill." – Exodus 20:13

So, if the Bible does clarify that life starts in the womb and that murder is wrong, that must mean abortion is murder. Yes then, the Bible does talk about it.

Liberal: It is my choice and right!

Me: Abortion has never been about your "choice."

It's about escaping the consequences of your foolish choice by taking all choices and rights away from another human being that resides helpless in your womb.

Liberal: We need Planned Parenthood because what happens if I get raped.

Me: Most abortions occur because one had sex before marriage and is simply too lazy to take care of the child. But sure, let's talk about the less than 1% of abortions.

"The fathers shall not be put to death for the children, neither shall the children be put to death for the fathers: every man shall be put to death for his own sin." - Deuteronomy 24:16

There is your answer. No, abortion is not okay in a rape or incest situation. If you think you can't support your child, please just give him/her up for adoption instead of murdering the child. Why have we placed such a low value on human life? A child is irreplaceable.

Liberal: What if the baby is deformed or will be special needs?

Me: *"And the Lord said unto him, Who hath made man's mouth? or who maketh the dumb, or deaf, or the seeing, or the blind? have not I the Lord?"* – Exodus 4:11

Is it not God that made the child deformed? Now, I can't tell you why He did, but I assure you that God did for a reason.

"And we know that all things work together for good to them that love God, to them who are the called according to his purpose." – Romans 8:28

Liberal: What if someone had an abortion? Are they going to hell?

Me: *"If we confess our sins, he is faithful and just to* *forgive us our sins, and to cleanse us from all unrighteousness.*" – 1 John 1:9

Not necessarily. If they don't turn from their sins and refuse to ask Christ into their hearts, then yes. But if they do turn from their sin and follow Christ then their sins will be forgotten!

LGBT Issues

I think many outdoorsmen have come to accept homosexuality or ignore it. I know that all of us see it as weird and unnatural. When one sits down for thirty seconds and thinks about homosexuality and what it entails, I can't imagine one getting up thinking that it okay. It is absolutely perverted and against everything that is normal and right. Again, don't get me wrong. I love all people, but just not their sin. Yes, sin. Homosexuality is sin. It is actually committing several sins at once. So let's tackle this.

"For the invisible things of him from the creation of the world are clearly seen, being understood by the

things that are made, even his eternal power and Godhead; so that they are without excuse:

Because that, when they knew God, they glorified him not as God, neither were thankful; but became vain in their imaginations, and their foolish heart was darkened.

Professing themselves to be wise, they became fools, And changed the glory of the uncorruptible God into an image made like to corruptible man, and to birds, and fourfooted beasts, and creeping things.

Wherefore God also gave them up to uncleanness through the lusts of their own hearts, to dishonour their own bodies between themselves: Who changed the truth of God into a lie, and worshipped and served the creature more than the Creator, who is blessed for ever. Amen.

For this cause God gave them up unto vile affections: for even their women did change the natural use into that which is against nature: And likewise also the men, leaving the natural use of the woman, burned in their lust one toward another; men with men working that which is unseemly, and receiving in themselves that recompence of their error which was meet.

And even as they did not like to retain God in their knowledge, God gave them over to a reprobate mind, to do those things which are not convenient;" – Romans 1:20-28

I know that was quite a bit of reading, but that covers three different sins in that context. The first is atheism, which we already discussed. The second I believe is to be veganism and will talk about that later. The third, of course, is homosexuality. I do not find it a coincident that these three sins are put right next to each other. I believe they follow each other. I have found that most vegans are atheist and that a large sum of vegans are homosexuals. Anyway, I am going to break these verses down now.

"Because that, when they knew God, they glorified him not as God, neither were thankful; but became vain in their imaginations, and their foolish heart was darkened.

AN OUTDOORSMAN'S HEART

Even though it is common sense that there is a God, they still denied Him and his glory. They are not thankful for any of God's creation and turn against the natural uses that He gave us, His creation. Their minds became perverted as their hearts turned to sin. Like veganism and homosexuality.

"Professing themselves to be wise, they became fools, And changed the glory of the uncorruptible God into an image made like to corruptible man, and to birds, and fourfooted beasts, and creeping things."

Vegans and gays profess themselves to be wise and right. It is their way or the highway. They command you to accept their perverted behavior and will stop at nothing until their sins are accepted. Vegans claim their way will save the planet, meanwhile we hunters know that conservation is the way to keep wildlife abundant. They changed the glory of God and turned to animals and man. They changed God to animals. They worship animals and think them higher than human life and God. Gays turned to corruptible man to do that which is unseemly.

"Wherefore God also gave them up to uncleanness through the lusts of their own hearts, to dishonour their own bodies between themselves: Who changed the truth of God into a lie, and worshipped and served the creature more than the Creator, who is blessed for ever. Amen."

God then gave them up into their sin and let them have their way. They were then dishonorable to their bodies, which is referring to a weak diet of eating only plants and having a physical relationship with the same gender. They changed the truth into a lie. The rainbow was a sign of God that represents his promises right after the great flood. Now, they have turned it into a lie representing the unimaginable. They changed the purpose of God's great outdoors into some cult group saying that it shouldn't be touched, and that wildlife has animal's rights. They choose to worship the animal instead of an almighty God.

"For this cause God gave them up unto vile affections: for even their women did change the natural use into that which is against nature: And likewise also the men, leaving the natural use of the woman, burned in their lust one toward another; men with men working that which is unseemly, and receiving in themselves that recompence of their error which was meet.

And even as they did not like to retain God in their knowledge, God gave them over to a reprobate mind, to do those things which are not convenient;"

God then gave them to their ways and vile affection, which is homosexuality. Man with man and woman with woman doing what is against nature. God doesn't want to see or even imagine that sin, so

God left the sin there to destroy us.

Pretty dark stuff guys. This is what humanity has come down to, changing that which was perfect into some perverted nastiness. Oh, how I mourn for this nation and knowing that God has left us. We will destroy ourselves by our own abominations. How dark have our hearts gotten?

If you know the story of Sodom and Gomora, then you know what homosexuality's judgment is. Sodom and Gomora were two cities that were mighty, just like this nation, that were full of homosexuality. Lot, the nephew of Abraham, was residing in these cities with his family. One day, the city guards and men broke into Lot's home demanding for this and that. Lot offered his daughter to the men. However, the men denied his daughter and requested his son... yep, going to stop there. That is how nasty this city was.

Well, God was so vexed with these cities he sought to destroy it. God told Abraham that if 50 people in the city were righteous, he would spare the city. After Abraham debated with God several times, God reduced the number of righteous people to 10. Ten people were not found so God's wrath was upon that city. There is not one trace of the cities today. Many believe that the Dead Sea is where the cities were. Which would mean, that God's wrath was so fierce on the cities that it created the deepest place on earth and a lake that nothing can reside in! There you have it...

Gun Rights

The part y'all have been waiting for. Finally, a teenager that is all for guns. Why yes, yes I am! This nation's biggest debate is on guns. Granted, guns are not in the Bible and are not a spiritual issue, but they are a self-defense issue and a human rights issue.

According to my research, guns prevent anywhere from 800,000 to 3 million incidents a year. Also, guns are used as an instrument of murder about 8000 times a year. So, people with guns have saved, at the very least, 100 times more people than people murdered with guns. Wow! Ended that debate, that should be the end of it, right? Apparently not, it seems the left think that is a gun issue not a people issue. If you go over to the U.K., where they have banned guns, they are now trying to ban pocketknives due to the uprising of murders with them. No matter what weapon you ban, the evil in man's heart will remain and they will go on to use another instrument to accomplish their agenda. Take a look at Chicago, they have the strictest gun rules in the nation and yet have the worst murder rate in the nation. Banning guns is not the answer.

A good guy with a gun is a great thing. If there is a bad guy in the room, his plan has just been spoiled, as there is now an increased chance of the bad guy getting shot. It is pretty simple logic.

Let's say they do ban guns somehow, even though the right is not to be infringed. All the good guys will turn in their guns like the law-abiding citizens they are. Meanwhile, the bad guys will not. What criminal obeys the law and why would they obey this law that strips them from accomplishing more crimes? More great logic. And now, the good guys don't have guns anymore and the bad guys can do their job easier! Okay, fine! The criminal's guns somehow all vanish. Then they will just move on to using another instrument. I just don't understand how one's logic can be so misplaced.

"A well-regulated militia being necessary to the security of a free state, the right of the people to keep and bear arms shall not be infringed." – The Second Amendment

The second amendment clearly states that it is an absolute necessity to have a military for this great nation, which is true. Because of that, the American people have the right to bear arms to protect themselves against the tyranny of the government. Our forefathers knew these days would come. No, not the great technology we have but that the government would come to what it is today. They predicted the fact that one day the government would seek to take away our guns. The best part is that my generation is pleading for the government to take away our rights. The forefathers wrote, "shall not be infringed" and yet it is being infringed. The forefathers wrote that amendment so that the people would have the same weaponry that the government has and yet we don't. The government's greatest weapon is likely the nuke; meanwhile we the people's deadliest arm is a 12-gauge shotgun and an AR-15. So yes, our rights have been stripped away from under our very noses without protest. It is an interesting thought and they will continue stripping away what little firepower we now have.

RACISM

Really this is the only issue most liberals and I can agree on. Racism is wrong. Period! No excuses. I couldn't care less what color skin you have. We are all created equal. However, this is where me and liberals break off again. I think they exaggerate racism in this country. Liberals can make every single thing anything says racist. It absurd. When something happens, they twist it and make it racist. I can comfortably say that not one American person today was a slave or owned a slave. We can't move forward if we keep living in the past. Plus, it was us conservative republicans that fought for their freedom and I am proud of that. You're welcome, so please stop calling me and all my friends racist because we are not. Now yes, there are a few nut jobs out there that are white supremacists but there also black supremacists. Both are in the wrong. My favorite fishing buddy is black. He doesn't care that I call him black and I don't care when he calls me a stubby white boy. Why don't we care? Because it is both true! I am white, he is black. So, what? I don't care, get over it. Please stop making everything racist. They discriminate themselves! I don't care what color you are! Period!

Also, another issue I have is that it is okay to be proud for everything but being white. Like I said, my white heritage built this great nation and fought for the freedom of slaves. For that, I am deeply proud.

Check this out on Wikipedia…

WIKIPEDIA
The Free Encyclopedia

Black pride

From Wikipedia, the free encyclopedia

Black pride is a movement encouraging people to take pride in being black. Related movements include black nationalism, Black Panthers, Afrocentrism and Black supremacism.

The slogan has been used in the United States by African Americans to celebrate heritage and personal pride. The black pride movement is closely linked with the

Gay pride

From Wikipedia, the free encyclopedia

Gay pride or **LGBT pride** is the positive stance against discrimination and violence toward lesbian, gay, bisexual, and transgender (LGBT) people to promote their self-affirmation, dignity, equality rights, increase their visibility as a social group, build community, and celebrate sexual diversity and gender variance. Pride, as opposed to

Asian pride

From Wikipedia, the free encyclopedia

In the United States, **Asian pride** (also spelled **AZN pride**) is a positive stance to being Asian American. The term arose from influences of hip hop culture within Asian

White pride

From Wikipedia, the free encyclopedia

White pride is a slogan primarily used by white separatist, white nationalist, neo-Nazi and white supremacist organizations to signal their racist viewpoints.[3][4]

Sociologists Betty A. Dobratz and Stephanie L. Shanks-Meile identified "White Power!

THE BOY SCOUTS DILEMMA

The outdoor industry is undoubtedly the most conservative industry in this nation. What did you think would happen if this nation's number one outdoor educational program went all liberal on us? Really smart move "Boy Scouts"... glad y'all thought that out. A whole 3% of this nation is painfully gay and how many of those 3% of gays are outdoorsy, gay girls? The "Boy Scouts" lost over 425,000 troops over the name change. There are definitely not 425,000 gay, outdoorsy female children out there. Guess what? According to the *Northwest Indiana Times*, only 3,000 girls have joined the "Boy Scouts." Shot yourself in the foot "Boy Scouts." Also, most liberals can't afford the scouts program anyway. Wait! Isn't there a girl scouts program too?

COUNTRY MUSIC

Of course, this is no life or death issue, but country music is often discussed in the outdoor industry. I really don't know too many teens my age that like any country music, new or old. This is actually really sad because most country songs are pretty clean and have somewhat powerful lyrics. No, not the songs that talk about girls and dirt roads, but the ones that are emotional and talk about family. Also, country music really goes hand and hand with the outdoors and patriotism. You'll find a lot of country songs that sing about the outdoors and this great nation. Those are my favorite.

Let's talk about people who argue over new (pop) and old country music. It is just a waste of time and breath. Who cares what type of country music one listens too. I listen to both new and old. I like them both. I do, however, like the 1995 to 2005 country music era more than anything else. That is just my opinion, nothing more. Everyone has a different taste in music. It is not worth losing a friend or getting in a debate about how one thinks that country is too "popish."

My personal favorite is when it comes to Luke Bryan. That guy takes a lot of heat from his fellow hunters. Yes, Luke Bryan is a hunter and a good one indeed. It is amazing how many debates and posts I'll see calling Luke Bryan "gay," which he isn't as he currently has married to a woman! Instead of harassing Luke Bryan and his music, why don't you applaud him for singing about the outdoors to millions of people? In all reality, Luke Bryan's music is more old country than new. Listen to some of the new stuff, it will change your opinion on Luke. Again, not a big issue but I think it was worth bringing up!

Freedom of Speech

It seems to me that only liberals get to exercise this amendment to the fullest. Conservatives can hardly get away with anything that is controversial. As much as I am against hate speech, it is free speech. Now of course, the left turns everything we say into hate speech even though 99% of it isn't. Again, they also make everything racist.

One of my recent experiences with this is that I

posted a photoshopped image of Colin Kaepernick kneeling on a platform that has hundreds of dying soldiers holding it up.

Blake Alma
June 7 at 7:01pm

WOW! This is a powerful image...so glad our soldiers are dying so that these rich NFL stars can disrespect our nation and its flag.

Like   Comment   Share

Joel Woods, Tracy Durham and 2.5K others

48,934 Shares

AN OUTDOORSMAN'S HEART

As you can see, the post went viral. I posted this on my personal Facebook page and didn't necessarily think it would blow up the way it did. Well, it did blow up and people were screaming their heads off, calling me racist and a bunch of horrible things. If you see the image, you clearly see that I acknowledge the fact that they are exercising freedom of speech but are wasting it foolishly. That was my simple point. I don't care that the reason behind the kneeling is this or that, no matter what, it is entirely disrespectful to this nation to kneel during the anthem. Period. That is all that I meant by the post. Our veterans who have gone out to fight for this country are dying for us so that we can disrespect the anthem and flag? I simply don't understand how you can be okay with that. I do consider Kaepernick's "protesting" hate speech against our nation, but hate speech is free speech.

Anyway, if you go on my page and read the thousands of comments you will find that I am in the wrong for posting that. Even though posting that image is me practicing my freedom of speech, I am not allowed to because it offends the left. Wait what?

An Outdoorsman's Conservatism

So, if Kaepernick can kneel during the anthem that must mean that I can post that I find his actions ridiculous since we both live in a free country. I'm in the wrong here? It is very simple logic.

Only liberals are now allowed to have free speech because what I do is offensive. What if I told you I think killing a baby in the womb or seeing a parade on the streets celebrating their sin of homosexuality is offensive? So, my factual opinion doesn't matter to you. I can't have free speech, but you can even though we live in the same country. Since when do you have more rights than me? Aren't you trying to get rid of the rights like the right to bear arms? I am very confused. Let me tell you about meme I saw that held a story which will change everyone's life…

John is on the internet.
John sees something on the internet that offends him.
John moves on.
John is smart.
Be like John.
The End

AN OUTDOORSMAN'S HEART

You're welcome.

Another example is the Roseanne situation. Roseanne Barr made a foolish tweet. I think we can all agree with that. However, what she said was protected by the first amendment and she had a right to say that. Yes, it was cruel, and she made a huge mistake. *ABC* also had the right to fire her just like the NFL had the right to end the kneeling. Do I disagree with *ABC*'s decision? Absolutely, but do I care enough to start posting on social media how mad I am about it? No! I don't care enough, as it is not a relevant issue in my life or your life. Yes, liberals can exercise their free speech more then we can but when I get to heaven I am not going to care about a TV show. In my opinion, both party made a mistake. Roseanne shouldn't have said anything, and *ABC* shouldn't have fired her for that. They both, however, had an American right to do the things they did. Not to mention, how much money they will lose for cancelling that show.

One more example that ended up working out I say, is when Phil Robertson of *Duck Dynasty* spoke out against homosexuality on a *GQ* interview. I have had the pleasure of interviewing Phil and I obviously stand with Phil entirely. As you know, *A&E* fired Phil from the show for speaking out. Due to *Duck Dynasty* being mostly watched by conservatives, *A&E* decided to bring Phil back just a few days later due to the outrage by fans. Phil got fired for speaking truth and he has a biblical and American right to do so. Liberalism at its finest. Also, did you know that both *ABC* and *A&E* are owned by Disney?!?!

PRESIDENT DONALD J. TRUMP

I thought all hope was lost during the 2016 election. The polls were in Hillary Clinton's favor. I thought for sure she would be the next president of this mighty nation. Boy! Was I ever so glad to be so wrong! Election night came, and Trump won in an electoral votes landslide and became my president that January. I am unbelievably grateful to have a president who forsook his billionaire lifestyle to bring back this country's greatness. The leftist media has had their pity party. They constantly rag on him calling this and that.

As much as I love are president, he is no Christian. His past life can surely attest to that and he has not made a public statement that he has come to the saving grace of Jesus Christ. Nevertheless, he does stand up for Christian values today and acknowledges that God has blessed this country. For that, I am grateful. The president is also pro-life, pro-gun, pro-hunting, pro-freedom of speech, pro-small government, pro-peace, and pro-military. He is also willing to work nonstop for the American people despite all the hate he has fought through. There is no denying that he can be a harsh person, but doesn't that make for a great president? He isn't political and has given it his best to keep all the promises he had made. So, I stand with him as a proof member of the great basket of deplorables.

An Outdoorsman's Conservatism

Let's take a look at all of President Trump's accomplishments:

- 100% vote by UN Security Council to sanction North Korea.
- 41% decline in illegal southern border crossings.
- 97,482 illegal immigrant arrests, 70% convicted of additional crimes, 52,169 expelled.
- Adopted a resolute policy on Afghanistan.
- Advocated for practical tertiary education.
- Advocated for skills-based immigration policies.
- American companies now expanding rather than shipping jobs overseas.
- Announced sanctions targeting Iran's Revolutionary Guards.
- Appointed a Transportation Secretary who is modernizing air traffic control.

AN OUTDOORSMAN'S HEART

- Appointed an Education Secretary who is correcting abuses of Title IX.

- Appointed an EPA administrator who has rescinded over 30 regulations.

- Appointed an FDA director who is facilitating generic drug competition.

- Appointed an Interior Secretary to improve forest management and expand users of public lands.

- Approved the Keystone pipeline.

- Called for international support of Iranian protesters.

- Canceled school lunch program that failed to force children to eat unpopular foods.

- Constructed test models of the border fence.

- Convinced Japan and South Korea to increase defense spending.

- Convinced NATO members to honor minimum financial commitments.

- Decertified Iranian nuclear treaty and sent it to Senate as constitutionally required.

- Designated North Korea as a state-sponsor of terrorism.

- Eliminated prohibition on interstate health insurance sales.

- Ended abuses of the student loan forgiveness program.

- Ended forced provision of contraception by Catholic nunneries.

- Ended requirement for state funding of Planned Parenthood.

- Ended research into Y2K preparedness.

- Ended rule requiring employers to report pay data by gender and race.

- Expanded school-choice efforts.

- FCC has begun to dismantle unnecessary Internet "Neutrality" regulations.

- Foreign firms building plants and creating jobs in the U.S.

- Improved rules of engagement for military in combat situations.

- Initiated resistance "sue and settle" tactics against EPA.

- Initiated sanctions on Venezuelan dictatorship.

- Introduced regulatory budgeting requiring agencies to rescind two rules to issue a new one.

- ISIS bombing ramped up from about 20 to 500 or more airstrikes per week.

- ISIS ground campaign intensified; Raqqa captured, its fighters surrendering in large numbers.

- Issued a National Security Strategy.

- Leveraged U.S. contribution to UN budget to force 5% budget cut and reduce staffs.

- NLRB reversed rule making indirect employee control sufficient to be "joint employees."

- Nominated 60 judges, 21 confirmed, none yet denied.

- Nominated a new Fed chief.

- Nominated one Supreme Court judge, who was confirmed.

- Obtained release of Aya Hijazi after three years in Egyptian prison.

- Obtained release of Caitlan Coleman and husband from Haqqani.

- Obtained release of UCLA basketball players from China.

- Raised awareness of Opioid addiction crisis.

- Recognized Jerusalem as Israeli capital and announced plan to move U.S. embassy there.

- Reduced permanent staff in all Cabinet agencies except VA, HS and Interior.

- Reduced White House staff by 110.

- Repeal of ACA mandate included in tax change bill.

- Requested increased funding for missile defense in face of North Korean and Iranian threats.

- Rescinded (temporarily) the Jones Act, facilitating speedier emergency shipments to Puerto Rico.

- Rescinded 2015 Waters of the United States rule.

- Rescinded ban drilling in the Arctic and coastal areas.

- Rescinded coal mining ban on public lands.

- Rescinded criminalization of accidental killing of migratory birds.

- Rescinded Cuban cash give-away.

- Rescinded the "Clean Power Plan."

- Rescinded the "War on Coal."

- Rescinded threat to pull funds from schools that prohibit transgenders picking their bathrooms.

- Rescinded Title IX "guidance letter" on sexual harassment.

- Restored policy barring federal funding of abortions overseas.

- Restoring military capability in the face of personnel shortages and equipment failures.
- Revamped U.S. space program, assigning ambitious new objectives.
- Revised rules for screening potential terrorist tourists.
- Sanctioned Venezuela for human rights violations.
- Sanctuary cities legislation passed House; pending in Senate.
- Signed 74 legislative bills (13 reversing executive orders) and 23 joint resolutions into law.
- Signed comprehensive tax change bill containing most of the changes he proposed.
- Signed legislation opening Arctic Natural Wildlife Reserve [ANWR] to oil drilling.
- Signed legislation to expedite firing of incompetent VA officials.
- Supreme Court largely upheld ban on selected travelers.

- Taking steps to control the rogue Consumer Finance Protection Agency.
- Targeted MS13 gang members for priority deportation.
- The president's lawyers announced a framework for restoring the separation of powers:
  - Congress should cease delegating its legislative power to the executive branch.
  - Courts should stop rubber-stamping regulations and orders that lack force of law.
  - Executive will end informal "guidance documents" that undermine due process.
- U.S. energy production is on the upswing.
- U.S. sorties and assisted forces reduced ISIS to 2% of the area controlled in 2016.
- Unemployment is at 4.1 percent, a 17-year low.
- Withdrew from Paris Climate Accord.

- Withdrew from UNESCO (a warning to other wasteful, overstaffed UN agencies).

This list is from historynewsnetwork.org

After reading all of that, how in the world could one not call Trump a great president? This list of accomplishments has been made in less than 500 days of his presidency too! Not even mentioning all the North Korea problems he has solved. So, thank you President Trump for making this nation great once more!

HOW MOST LIBERALS WILL READ THIS BOOK...

There are some, but not many, who are civil and acknowledge the good things that Trump has done. In fact, I have a few liberal fishermen friends and we get along like we are best friends. I have even received support from liberals saying that they like what I am doing. Hence, not all liberals are unfriendly to us! If liberals acted as mature as these folks mentioned above, I wouldn't be writing this now.

AN OUTDOORSMAN'S HEART

But most will not receive this as constructive criticism. They will take it as hate and then discriminate themselves and call me a racist or a homophobe. Yadda, yadda, yadda… well, I am not and if you were capable of reading anything I wrote thus far, you would know that I am not. I want to write this all-in kindness just as Christ would do. I hope that I can articulate all of this simply and kindly.

You will likely see book reviews that are negative, stating that I am a nutjob or that I have a mental disorder. The only reason I know this is because I have gotten reviews like that before. Most liberals will not take this well as all truth hurts. People have told me things that are true and I denied them because they hurt. I understand that. You can't get all bent out of shape when someone provides you with constructive criticism and you react by acting like a four-year-old by calling them this or that. If you civilly reacted and share your side of views, I admire that. I read almost all the comments on my social media. Most liberal comments insult me by calling me a whatever and when they do that they lose all credibility with me. Their opinion becomes meaningless when they act like a toddler. When they civilly make a point and state their side of view with kindness, then I like their comment, reply with acknowledging their kindness, and respectfully agreeing or disagreeing. If every liberal acted kindly, maybe your opinions would be more respected. When Hollywood says "*Blank* Trump," their opinion goes right out the window. Don't be this way, but be kind. Make your statement, agree or disagree, and move on. Simple…

CHAPTER 6:

AN OUTDOORSMAN'S HARASSMENT

If you know anything about me, I obviously have a burning passion for all things outdoors. Fishing, with no doubt is my favorite, but hunting has this soul satisfying attribute I can never describe. The outdoors revolutionizes someone's life.

"Immerse yourself in the outdoor experience, it will cleanse your soul and make you a better person."

– Fred Bear, the father of modern bowhunting

I know I mentioned this amazing quote already, but it's worth bringing up again because it is entirely true. I know so because it has done so. The outdoors has prompted me to do so many things. No, not just my career, but my lifestyle and how I live my life. Keeping busy in the awe of God's creation keeps me from sin and being immersed in the ways of this sinful world. There is no denying that living an outdoor lifestyle gives you higher morals. However, the outdoors is just a temporary soul cleanser. Christ is the eternal soul cleanser!

This being understood by all outdoorsmen, that which is good always brings in evil. Evil took the incorruptible image of God and turned into the image of animals. They, being antihunters and vegans, took something that represented God and turned it into some sort of cult, a hypocritical animal loving cult.

Anyone who hunts has run into people who are against hunting. That could either be a very hypocritical antihunter with a cheeseburger in his hands or a vegan who thinks they are better than everyone else. If you have read any of my other books, you know then that I have already tackled this topic by writing *The Hunter's War*. I will be using the same excerpts from my book in this chapter. Why rewrite a master piece? Just kidding. This chapter will be focused on handling the backlash we get from these people.

When I was 14-years-old, I would set up several modified rat traps to trap squirrels for both meat and fur. I accidentally ended up trapping a chipmunk instead. I, feeling sorry for the unwanted kill, decided to use its death for good use. I ended up skinning it and salting the skin. After the skin was dried, I decided I would use its hide as a bookmark for my recently published book, *The Outdoorsmen Bible*.

I ended up writing a how-to-do article for instructables.com about the chipmunk bookmark. I showed the reader how to trap the chipmunk, skin it, and salt it. It was simple and fun. It was published, and I received about 100 hate messages during the first day of its publication. This was my very first time ever experiencing anti-hunters. It discouraged me at my super young age. My most hurtful hate comment was the following: "My only wish is to fill your skull with molten aluminum, and hammer your fingers alive, and drill your teeth with a strong driller...I'm serious, cause you're a bad and useless creature (unfortunately). Even though 'creature' is much for you, then let's say you are 'some juxtaposed atoms taking up space.'"

THE CREATION OF ANIMALS

"In the beginning God created the heaven and the earth.

And God said, Let the waters bring forth abundantly the moving creature that hath life, and fowl that may fly above the earth in the open firmament of heaven. And God created great whales, and every living creature that moveth, which the waters brought forth abundantly, after their kind, and every winged fowl after his kind: and God saw that it was good. And God blessed them, saying, Be fruitful, and multiply, and fill the waters in the seas, and let fowl multiply in the earth. And the evening and the morning were the fifth day.

*And God said, Let the earth bring forth the living creature after his kind, cattle, and creeping thing, and beast of the earth after his kind: and it was so. And God made the beast of the earth after his kind, and cattle after their kind, and every thing that creepeth upon the earth after his kind: and God saw that it was good. And God said, Let us make man in our image, after our likeness: and let them have **dominion** over the fish of the sea, and over the fowl of the air, and over the cattle, and over all the earth, and over every creeping thing that creepeth upon the earth. So God created man in his own image, in the image of God created he him; male and female created he them. And God blessed them, and God said unto them, Be fruitful, and multiply, and replenish the earth, and subdue it: and have dominion over the fish of the sea, and over the fowl of the air, and over every living thing that moveth upon the earth. And God said, Behold, I have given you every herb bearing seed, which is upon the face of all the earth, and every tree,* *in the which is the fruit of a tree yielding seed; to you it shall be for meat. And to every beast of the earth, and to every fowl of the air, and to every thing that creepeth upon the earth, wherein there is life, I have given every green herb for meat: and it was so. And God saw every thing that he had made, and, behold, it was very good. And the evening and the morning were the sixth day."*

Genesis 1 (KJV)

That is how God created the world, the animals, and mankind!

*And God said, Let us make man in our image, after our likeness: and **let them have dominion** over the fish of the sea, and over the fowl of the air, and over the cattle, and over all the earth, and over every creeping thing that creepeth upon the earth. So God created man in his own image, in the image of God created he him; male and female created he them.*

Genesis 1:16

God created man to control the animals, to have dominion over them, but what does dominion mean? Let's find out.

Definition of DOMINION
1: supreme authority
2: absolute ownership
Merriam-Webster Dictionary

How about that? God has given us absolute ownership and supreme authority over animals. Well that is cool, eh? Wait a second; a vegan may use this against you. However, we can put this to rest.

And God said, Behold, I have given you every herb bearing seed, which is upon the face of all the earth, and every tree, in the which is the fruit of a tree yielding seed; ***to you it shall be for meat***.

So, we can only eat veggies? (Yes, that is what I am calling them.) First off, veggies aren't meat, so why does the Bible call it meat? Well, veggies were the substitute for meat for the first 2000 years of history, until after the great flood. It was always planned by God for us to eat meat. Let's read Genesis 9:3.

Every moving thing that liveth (all animals) *shall be meat for you; even as the green herb have I given you all things.*

That verse replaces the verse back in chapter 1 of Genesis. Animals are the meat for you now, not veggies. Veggies are now just, well… veggies. Now you can be an omnivore, like me. For the past 4,000 years, we have been allowed by God to eat meat. I want you to remember these verses for the road up ahead.

WHY WERE ANIMALS CREATED?

What is the point and meaning to animal life? First off, animals don't have souls. When they die, they do not go to heaven or to hell. They go into the dirt. Back in Genesis 1:16, the Bible says we have complete dominion over the animals. This means we can use them to benefit our lives. They can be food, they can be sold, they can be slaves (like horses and cows), they can be pets, and they can be placed in zoos.

God created the animal for our own benefit. God created animals and plants for the man and God created man for Himself. I call that the *Circle of Life*. The purpose of an animal is to serve the man, as we are to serve the Creator.

So, there you have it! The Bible says animals can be hunted. There you go hunters! That is all you need to know about animal life and veganism. Boy, do I wish that was all you needed! Even though the Bible makes it clear, vegans will probably end up saying to you, "How dare you use the Bible to say you can kill animals. That disgusts me!" How would I know that? Because vegans have said that to me many times before.

I'd say about 99% of vegans are anti-Bible, so they think the Bible doesn't apply to them, and they will say whatever to make you change your mind. Most American vegans are atheist, meaning that they believe that we evolved from animals. What a joke. I will talk more about that later.

Let's say I have a gun to my head and I believe with all my heart, soul, and mind that the gun isn't there. Does that mean the gun isn't there? Of course not! By the time the trigger is pulled, it doesn't matter that I didn't believe that the gun was actually there, because it didn't do anything to save me. The same thing is applied to the Bible. I can believe with all my heart, soul, and mind that it isn't true, but by the time I am dead, what good did my unbelief do? Nothing.

Some vegans may say that they only believe parts of the Bible and, conveniently, they don't believe Genesis 9:3. Imagine having an instruction pamphlet showing you how to build a building block set. You decide you don't like or "believe" in a step, and you skip it. What happens? You finish the project, but it is all messed up because you only liked/believed part of the pamphlet. It is the same thing with the Bible. If there is only one thing wrong in the Bible, then it is all messed up. Henceforth, the Bible is not untrue because the Bible has proven itself to be correct throughout human history. The outdoors alone proves the Bible to be true as it says in Romans 1:20, my favorite Bible verse.

For the invisible things of him from the creation of the world (the outdoors) *are clearly seen, being understood by the things that are made, even his eternal power and Godhead; so that they are without excuse:*

PETS OR FOOD?

Eli and Aryanna Gourdin, a father/daughter-hunting duo (and former co-hosts of my radio show), have experienced the pain of anti-hunting criticism. Aryanna and her father went on a safari hunting trip to Africa. During her hunting trip in Africa, she legally pulled off shooting both a zebra and a giraffe. She kindly donated all the meat to the African tribes. I have personally been hunting game for years and I have never shot a trophy like that in my lifetime! I find her kill very impressive. Aryanna simply decided to post a picture her harvest on Facebook. Unfortunately, because of anti-hunters on the internet, she received many hate massages and even death threats! She received over 75,000 negative comments on her Facebook post and they are still counting. She has been called "sick" and an "animal hater." Aryanna has not recanted her hunting lifestyle. She has simply replied kindly and softly to this situation saying, "I will never back down from hunting, because I am a hunter!" Many outdoorsmen and supporters of Aryanna have stated, "Let the haters hate. Hunt away Aryanna!"

She has appeared all over the media because of this situation. She even appeared on "*Good Morning Britain.*" Piers Morgan, the host, asked Aryanna an odd question, "*On your Facebook page there are pictures of you cuddling your pet cat. Right? You love your little pet cat. How would you feel if I came to your house one day, and I hunted down your pet cat, and I killed it, and I then posted pictures of me celebrating the slaughter of your dead cat?*"

Why in the world would I hunt a pet? No hunter would just hunt a pet because they have the power to kill. That is one dumb question. God gave all animals a purpose! Some are for meat, some are for fur, some are for the conservation of plants and other animal species, and some are for pets.

WHAT IS A PET?

A pet is an animal kept primarily for a person's company and enjoyment. A pet is often a fun, playful, and friendly animal. Dogs, cats, birds, house rabbits, guinea pigs, hamsters, fish, turtles, hermit crabs, frogs, snakes, and lizards are common American pets. Some animals are designed by God to be human friends and to bring us enjoyment. Pets do this. I love pets. I would never hunt a pet. There would be no point in killing a pet, because it is not the purpose of pets to be hunted, instead they bring us joy and company.

Some animals are meant for beauty and for human interest. Zoo animals are a prime example of this. Zoo animals also bring us joy and happiness. Zoo animals are kept captive to help animals in need and to make money as a company. I personally love zoos.

Some animals are working animals (like horses, camels, and cows). Some are livestock. Some are even laboratory animals, which are kept primarily for performance, agricultural value, or research.

WHAT IS A GAME ANIMAL?

A game animal is an animal hunted for the purpose of meat, fur, or other animal products. There are hundreds of different species of game animals across the world. In America, perhaps the most known game species is the deer. Other American game animals include: elk, moose, black bear, grizzly bear, bison, mountain lion, coyote, foxes, raccoon, rabbits, squirrels, doves, turkey, pheasants, opossum, wild boar, bobcats, duck, geese, alligators, bull frogs, and even rattlesnakes. All the animals I have just listed are edible animals. Some are often hunted or trapped for fur or other animal products. God designed game animals for the purpose of meat or animal products. They are not designed to be pets but are designed for human gain.

THE PET LOVER AND ANIMAL LOVER

There is a huge difference between a pet lover and an animal lover. I am an animal lover. Some may just be pet lovers. Let me explain this to you.

An animal lover is one who loves all animals for their designated purposes. Game animals are for resources. Pets are for company. Zoo animals are for enjoyment. Working animals are for ease of work. Others are for conservation of plants. I love game animals, I love pets, I love zoo animals, I love working animals, and all the other animals. No matter what the animal's purpose is, I love it and I will not take it for granted.

A pet lover is one who loves all animals for only one purpose, to be looked at and "enjoyed." They may not know this, but they think of all animals as "pets." That would make game animals absolutely pointless. Game animals are not pets. They are not designed to be played with like a dog. They are designed to benefit the man with its God-given resources. A pet lover looks at all animals to be taken for granted. This is my point of view on these two terms.

Vegans and anti-hunters are pet lovers. Hunters are generally animal lovers. Hunters love pets and game animals in two different ways. Vegans love animals for one reason: just to be gazed upon. That would give the majority of animals no purpose of life.

As you can see, there are many different purposes for animals. Some are for pets, and some are for food. Don't let anti-hunters say that all animals are to be left untouched. That is wasting the creation of God.

UNDERSTANDING VEGANISM

To be quite frank, there is really no hunter who "understands" veganism. However, I want you to understand what it is, and why it is so wrong.

Don't get me wrong; I actually love vegans and anti-hunters, as I love all people. I just don't like their belief of veganism. A HUGE and VERY COMMON mistake that most people make is the difference between a vegan and a vegetarian! You must understand the difference between the two in order to realize what is so wrong with veganism.

A vegetarian is one who eat doesn't eat MEAT because of health issues, or because they don't like the flavor of it. Vegetarians use animal products. They eat eggs. They drink milk. There is absolutely nothing wrong with being a vegetarian because they choose not to eat meat for their own reasons, and they typically have no problems with hunters and trappers.

Once again, a vegan is one who doesn't eat meat because they believe that animals have a higher calling. Vegans use NO animal products. However, some vegans may drink milk. Vegans sometimes classify milk as animal "waste." Sometimes vegans will contradict themselves. Generally, a vegan will believe that animal life is greater than human life because we "evolved" from them. This is not the case with all vegans. However, vegans show an unnecessary care, love, and emotion for all animals!

Let also clarify, that a lot of vegetarians all

themselves vegans when they don't actually hold true vegan values. Be sure you identify why they are vegan before assuming they hate hunters. I have made that mistake far too many times.

For instance, here in my hometown of Cincinnati, a three-year-old boy climbed into a gorilla habitat at the Cincinnati Zoo and was grabbed and dragged by Harambe, a gorilla. Fearing for the young boy's life, a zookeeper shot and killed Harambe, which was a wise call. The incident was recorded on video and was aired all over the mainstream media. It caused anger and havoc all across the world, not because of the boy falling into the habit, but because the gorilla was killed. Conservationists wrote later that the zoo had no other choice under the circumstances, of which I agree with. Vegans and some anti-hunters, of course, were very livid about this situation.

Let me talk about this for a moment. First off, I would kill every single gorilla in the world to save any one human of any race. Yes, you heard me! Second off, what good does a gorilla do for the human race outside of being locked up in a zoo?

Absolutely nothing! So, who cares about the death of an animal that has no huge and significant cause to the human race! Apparently, vegans do! Sure, it is sad that the gorilla had to die, but they had no choice. The zoo keepers put the life of the human above the life of the dangerous animal. Human life is far greater than any animal life. One human is greater than the life of all the animals combined! Remember all animals were created by God for us, and we are created in the image of God for God!

Some may say the gorilla was protecting the child. Ok sure... NOT! The only thing the boy needed to be protected from is the gorilla. My funny opinion is that animal activists base this thought on the very fictional *Disney* movie, *Tarzan*. Dumb, right? Gorillas kill for sport! I am 100% sure that the gorilla would have killed the boy if the zoo hadn't killed the gorilla first. So, vegans should hate gorillas because they kill for sport. They shouldn't hate us. Hundreds and hundreds of animal species kill for sport! Why don't vegans get mad at other animals for killing for sport, eh? Because they treasure and love animal life far over human life. This is just one example of veganism.

Today, there are many movies and TV shows about animals that have the minds and knowledge like humans do and this is fine. Somehow movies about animals have some influence on vegans that animals have some higher calling than us. For the past 5,900 years, veganism has NEVER been a problem. I am convinced that modern fictional animal movies had some influence on veganism.

The question is, why do vegans love animals so much? Apparently, they think they have a higher calling than to serve man. The only higher calling than serving man is to serve God, and that is our own privilege. Animals do not serve God! Animals do not have souls. Animals are only designed to help the man in order to help the man serve God. Again, it is the circle of life.

Let me step off the vegan train here and let's talk a bit about anti-hunters and animal activists. Anti-hunters and animal activists can be vegans, but most of them actually eat meat and use animal products. So why do they have so much "love" for animal life? The truth is I really don't know because it doesn't make any sense to me. However, I can take a pretty good guess. My guess is that they want to be noticed and want some attention. Even though they are hypocritical, they just want people to notice them and say, "They must be good people because they take care of animals." No, they don't! They eat meat and use animal products just like you and me. However, if an animal activist or an anti-hunter doesn't eat meat and doesn't use animal products, I would classify them as a vegan. I describe animal activist, anti-hunters, and vegans as different types of people. Vegans are animal activists on steroids.

TREE HUGGERS

Someone once asked me, "How do you feel about tree huggers?" I chuckled at that question. My outdoorsy viewpoint on tree huggers is that they are just outdoorsmen gone bad. I would put a tree hugger in the animal activist category, unless they don't eat meat, then again, I would classify them as a vegan. A tree hugger is one who protects and loves all wildlife at an extreme measure. I love and protect wildlife too, but not at extreme measures. Remember, I love animal life for all of their purposes. Tree huggers only love animals to be just looked at and passed by, which is biblically incorrect. Some animals are just for enjoyment while others are for food and animal products. Tree huggers generally place wildlife (plants and animals) over human life.

VEGANS AREN'T ANY BETTER THAN HUNTERS!

All humans are sinners, first off. Second off, let's talk about the ultimate American reason why vegans treasure animal life over human life. Atheism!

If vegans believe in evolution, that would make them much worse than any hunter. How so? Let me start off with this. If there is no God, then there is no Bible. If there is no Bible, there is no LAW! The laws of man are built upon the very foundations of the Bible. If there is no God, there is no devil, meaning there is no right or wrong. If there is no right or no wrong, that would mean I could go around killing anything I want. So, who cares kills if I go around animals then, O vegan?

Then why do we have a conscience? Because there is a God who put it into our heads! However, the vegan generally believes that there is no God. Again, that would put a hunter at no fault then and that would also put the vegan at no fault.

Vegans are vegans because they believe that we humans evolved from animals. Henceforth, we shouldn't eat them because that is where we came from. Where did the animals come from? Plants! And what do vegans only eat? Plants. So, if evolution is true, that would mean that vegans are only eating the very original source that we originated from. This puts them at more fault than hunters because they only eat the original source that humans and animals originated from. Hypocrites! Vegans get a taste of their own medicine, eh? However, this chunk of truth would be irrelevant if there was no God. But there is, henceforth making vegans very hypocritical, which is against the law of the Bible.

A vegan will not eat eggs. An egg is an offspring

of a chicken. However, vegans obviously eat fruits and vegetables. Fruits and vegetables are offspring of a plant. Again, being hypocritical.

The vegan will tell you that animals and plants are very different. We have already talked about how a vegan feels about animals because of their atheist belief. Again, vegans contradict themselves. The fact is that if evolution were true, plants would be more "important" because they were here first. If that doesn't work for a vegan, they will say that animals have a nervous system meanwhile plants don't. Even though that is a true statement, it really doesn't prove anything nor does it change anything. Why? God created animals with nervous systems for our own human benefit. God gave animals nervous systems because without a nervous system how can they have locomotion and how can they eat? If pets and zoo animals couldn't move, how can they bring joy and company to us? If game animals don't have hunger pains, how can they gain muscle for us to eat? Heck, how could they even live? Again, this just proves a hunter's point further.

AN OUTDOORSMAN'S HEART

Other than the nervous system, animals and plants are the exact same thing. They can both breathe, eat, move (plants grow, which is "moving"), reproduce, and they both have cells. Hence, there is no "greater than" between plants and animals.

That would put vegans at committing two sins. One is putting animal life over God and humans. The second is being hypocritical. Romans 1:25 says:

Who changed the truth of God into a lie, and worshipped and served the creature (animals) *more than the Creator, who is blessed for ever. Amen.*

We have talked about how the creation of the world proves the evidence of a Creator, and now 5 verses later we have this. Vegans have turned the truth of God into lie (creation to evolution), and they have chosen to love and worship the animal over the Creator.

POACHING

I am 100% against poaching! Not because of the poacher killing the animal, but because he is disobeying the law. Poaching is the illegal act of killing animals. There are laws in the United States protecting endangered animals, protecting the overkilling of an animal species (like deer), and for human safety.

For instance, here in Butler County, Ohio I am legally limited to hunting two deer per a hunting season. Why? Because the government does not want the deer population to become too thin. As hunters, we must obey the laws or else we are at fault.

WHY IS VEGANISM A SUCH BIG DEAL?

As a hunter, it is frustrating to deal with anti-hunters. To us outdoorsmen, veganism is a huge deal. But what does the everyday person think about it? I'd say that most people are on the fence about this situation. But I don't think too many people find veganism that big of a deal. Again, it is a big deal.

Vegans have hate toward us hunters because we hunt game animals. What does the Bible say about hate?

Ye have heard that it was said of them of old time, Thou shalt not kill; and whosoever shall kill shall be in danger of the judgment: But I say unto you, That whosoever is angry with his brother without a cause shall be in danger of the judgment: and whosoever shall say to his brother, Raca (translated I hate you), shall be in danger of the council...
~Matthew 5:21-22a

Veganism is hate toward a hunter without a cause. There is no reason for a vegan to be angry at a hunter because they legally hunt animals as the Bible allows. Having hate or unnecessary anger toward another person is murder. Vegans have murdered then. I have murdered then, too. It is wrong for a hunter to hate a vegan back. However, we must still love the vegan but not the sin.

The death of an animal is so minimal compared

to other important matters in this world. The media makes a huge deal about animals who are killed for game. Why? Because it brings anger to people for absolutely no reason, and it gets the reader or viewer to view the program. That makes media some serious ad sales! I know this because I have ad sales with my own show, I know how media works. The media companies couldn't care less about the death of the animal. They just want the big bucks! (No pun intended.)

The media knows something that we don't really think of too often. The media often tells you things that really don't matter, like big game hunting, pointless political issues, and celebrity junk. They generally don't make a huge deal about the things we should really be worried about. Things like Isis, abortion, human murder, inner city crimes, wars, LGBT rights, rising socialism, and just the thought that billions of people don't know about Jesus. That is what we should be worried about. But not the death of animals that have little human value, like a gorilla or giraffe. There are other things in this decaying world for us to worry about. Who cares about the death of animal when all these other things are going on? It may be sad to you to watch an animal die, but do you know what makes me sadder? The death of a fellow Christian getting his head chopped off by ISIS. Yeah, I am a little more worried about that than a dead gorilla. Thankfully, Trump has nearly eradicated all of ISIS. Animal activists get more upset over the death of an animal than the death of an innocent baby in the womb or an elderly man getting shot while walking down the street. I am sorry, I have other things to worry about. I am actually really not sorry. Think about that…

HEALTH

All animal meat contains huge sums of protein. Meat and milks contain the highest content of protein in the human diet. Protein is like gas for a car, but for a human. Protein is what builds muscle. Your strength comes from protein. If you are strong and bulked like me, (not really…) it is because your body has enough protein to build up that muscle. Fruits and veggies contain very little protein. Vegans are generally much slimmer than meat eaters and vegans have very little muscle tissue.

Maria Strydom, a vegan mountain climber, wanted to prove to the world that vegans can do anything if they put their heart into it. Maria practiced and prepared non-stop for the ultimate trek. She was determined to climb Mount Everest. She wanted to prove to all that a vegan has the same physical capability to climb the 29,029-foot mountain as a meat eater. She continued pursuing this goal. The day came when she was "ready" to make this treacherous trek. Unfortunately, she lacked the physical capability to do so and sadly she died while trying to climb Mount Everest.

Even though that story is a terribly sad one, it should not be overlooked. Vegans lack the protein and strength to do the things that meat eaters can. This is another error of veganism.

STANDING UP

Well outdoorsman, I hope this chapter thus far has helped you understand the importance of hunting and the foolishness of veganism. Now it is your job to defend your right to bear arms and the right to hunt. I cannot fight for you, but I sure will try. Trust me, writing this book will just make animal activists hate me more because they know this is true, but they don't want to believe such things.

Outdoorsman, I want you to ask yourself why you are a hunter or trapper. Here is why I am a hunter and why I love the outdoors:

- It gives me free Food!
- I get fur that makes me some money.
- It is a fun hobby.
- It is a fun profession.
- I make a living directly from the outdoors.
- It proves evidence of a God.
- It shows the glory and power of God.

- It is what all life lives off of. All food and resources come from the outdoors!
- God created the outdoors for our own enjoyment and pleasure. God also created animals to be meat for us.
- It strengthens me physically, mentally, and spiritually.
- As I see the wonders of my Creator, it brings me happiness.

Job 37:14 - *Hearken unto this, O Job: stand still, and consider the wondrous works of God.*

For these reasons, I am an outdoorsman and I will always be one. Nobody will tell me otherwise. I encourage you to stand up for your rights to hunt, and not to let people try to take it away because THEY think it is wrong while the Creator has allowed us to do such a thing.

CHAPTER 7:

AN OUTDOORSMAN'S FAITH

As I draw nigh to an end, I think about my role in outdoors. Is it to be a voice of reason to the American outdoorsman? Or to be a motivator to get kids back outdoors? Maybe, but one thing is for certain; my faith will never leave me on this journey. While my future is uncertain, I know for a fact that I will never stop believing in God, and that this nation can be great once more. A day may come where I am beat and torn, but I will never forget the words I have written in this book.

The greatest event in my life was not when I experienced the outdoors for the first time. It was the day I came to know Christ. July 29th, 2010, I came to know the gospel. I was 9 years old at a small Christian junior camp. That evening there was speaker who asked a very simple question. "Do you know if you died tonight where you would spend eternity?" Even though it wasn't necessarily that blunt, it still struck my mind. The evening service was coming to an end and he asked everyone to close his eyes and bow his head. I did so. He then said, "If you are not sure if you are going to one day go to heaven, raise your hand." I did that too. My counselor, Chris Young, took me back to the boy's dorm and asked me several questions regarding my salvation. After a long chat, I concluded that I wasn't saved. That night, I prayed and simply asked God to take away my sins. I asked Him to forgive my sins and told Him I believe that He sent His only Son to die on the cross for my sins and rose again three days later. It was that simple. That night, this outdoorsman's heart came to the saving grace of Jesus Christ!

Everything I have written in this book is because of one God, the person who created the entire outdoors and me. The one who made all thing possible. Jesus Christ! Now, may I share with you the most important thing, not only in this book, but also in the world?

We all must realize that we are all sinners, including me. Romans 3:10 says, "As it is written, there is none righteous, no, not one."

We will all die because of our sin. Romans 6:23 "For the wages of sin is death......"

No one can make up for their sin with good works. Nothing we do will earn our way to heaven – not good works, not church membership, not baptism, NOTHING! Ephesians 2:8-9 *"For by grace are ye saved through faith; and that not of yourselves: it is the gift of God: Not of works, lest any man should boast."*

There is only one way to heaven – turning from our sin (repentance) and putting our faith in Jesus Christ. John 14:6 *"Jesus saith unto him, I am the way, the truth, and the life: no man cometh unto the Father, but by me."*

You are correct if you realize this is a very narrow way to heaven. In fact, the Bible agrees with you. Matthew 7:14 "...*Strait is the gate, and narrow is the way, which leadeth unto life, and few there be that find it."* The only way to heaven is through Jesus Christ – faith in His death on the cross, His burial and His resurrection from the dead! Most of us know John 3:16, but most do not know John 3:18 which says, *"He that believeth on him is not condemned: but he that believeth not is condemned already, because he hath not believed in the name of the only begotten Son of God."*

The evidence that someone is truly a Christian is a dramatically changed life - not a perfect life, but a life that is dedicated to Jesus Christ.

II Corinthians 5:17 says, *"Therefore if any man be in Christ, he is a new creature: old things are passed away; behold, all things are become new."*

Let the atheist scoff. Let the vegan insult me. Let the

liberal cry out against me. And let the homosexual pronounce me as a homophobic for I am not ashamed of the gospel of Christ!

Here's my outdoorsman's heart, oh, take and seal it.
Seal it for Thy courts above.

Epilogue:

An Outdoorsman's Legacy

After the few years of working in the outdoor industry, I have been applauded for my young age and my labor. I have always seen age simply as a number. I never thought my age would be one of the biggest factors of my work. Being called the future of the outdoors and the forerunner of next generation of outdoorsmen has been unbelievably humbling. Quite frankly, I am not the future of the outdoors. I am just one of many outdoor youngsters trying to help the industry. I, working in media, made it easier for people to find me. Most of my fellow outdoor peers work behind the scenes. I thought I would name a few kids that hold the future of the outdoors.

- **Jackson Hartley** (age 15), founder of Younghuntr.com.

- **Andy Hicks** (age 19), founder of Central Missouri Outdoors.

- **Alli Armstrong** (age 19), co-host *of Grace, Camo, and Lace* on Sportsman Channel.

- **Adriana Armstrong** (age 15), co-host of *Grace, Camo, and Lace* on Sportsman Channel.

- **Dan Olmstead** (age 15), founder of Olmstead Outdoors.

- **Dylan Jackson** (age 19), founder of Tagged Out Calls.

- **Aryanna Gourdin** (age 12), hunting martyr and former co-host of *The Outdoorsman's Art Radio Show*.

- **Nevin Burns** (age 8), founder of Nevin's Hunting Friends.

- **Kendall Jones** (age 19), hunting martyr and activist.

These are just of the few fellow youngsters I personally know that are trying to make difference. The ages next to their names are the time of life that they started making their difference to my knowledge.

There is a great comfort to me that I am not the only kid trying to revive the outdoor world and bringing it to the next generation. Sure, I may be the loudest of them all and perhaps their forerunner, but they are the ones who will make the real difference. I only hope that I can inspire them to stand up for their God-given rights and be an ambassador of the outdoors.

I alone cannot carry this burden for my generation. I know not when my road will end. For when my bank account runs dry or when a godless character carries out their death wish, my outdoorsman's legacy will go on.

About the Author:

Blake Alma is an award-winning writer, TV & radio host, and published author. He hosts and produces *The Outdoorsman's Art Radio Show* and *The Outdoor Experience TV* on Hunt Channel. Blake loves and pursues the outdoors and its Creator with all that he has. Some of Blake's favorite outdoor activities include fishing, survival, trapping, hunting, and camping.

The
Outdoor Experience
with Blake Alma

HUNT CHANNEL

▶ **MONDAYS** AT **10PM** ET

OutdoorExperienceTV.com